GROWING A GROUP

W9-DBU-682

Roots of Youth Ministry Series

This series addresses ecumenical and uniquely Presbyterian youth ministry concerns. Volumes in this series are intended for both professional and lay adults engaged in youth ministry.

Series Writers

Rodger Nishioka
Bob Tuttle
Lynn Turnage

Series Editor

Faye Burdick

Titles In Series

GROWING A GROUP

LYNN TURNAGE

Bridge Resources
Louisville, Kentucky

Edited by Faye Burdick

Book interior and cover design by Pamela Ullman

First edition

Published by Bridge Resources
Louisville, Kentucky

Web site address: http://www.bridgeresources.org

PRINTED IN THE UNITED STATES OF AMERICA

98 99 00 01 02 03 04 05 06 07 — 10 9 8 7 6 5 4 3 2 1

Library of Congress Cataloging-in-Publication Data

Turnage, Lynn, date.
   Growing a group / Lynn Turnage —1st ed.
     p. cm. — (Roots of youth ministry series)
   Includes bibliographical references.
   ISBN 1-57895-012-0
   1. Church group work with youth. I. Title. II. Series.
BV4447.T86 1998
259'.23—dc21   98-6791

To Mom and Dad

Contents

Acknowledgments

The annual Recreation Workshop takes place in May in Montreat, North Carolina. It is at this workshop that I've enjoyed, learned, absorbed, stolen, borrowed, adapted, witnessed, created, and been challenged and rejuvenated. I've also been encouraged in my leadership and stretched to think, play, and experience the love of Christ in the community of faith. I am grateful to the leadership and participants of this conference for continually challenging and encouraging me.

During college, I worked a summer in the Club Program in Montreat. It was one of the best jobs that I ever had. This day-camp program has the privilege of having the entire town of Montreat as its playground. The programs and ideas I learned there as a college student still continue to draw me—games whose only limit was our own creativity. There were places to explore, to ask questions, and to *be* yourself, as well as opportunities to experience God.

Another source of inspiration is my friend and colleague in recreation—Eve Carriker. I'm grateful to her for prompting me to look for and to try the new and different, and for continuing to push me to be more of the person God created me to be. Eve prodded and asked questions and encouraged me to find the "hows" and "whys," as well as to find words to explain how and where the Holy Spirit moves in God's re-creations.

Glenn Bannerman continues to be my mentor. He is the master of moving people in and out of groups, nonchalantly working with the Holy Spirit as it moves among and in individuals and groups. I continue to learn from just watching him work with a group.

My other recreation friends get special thanks, too. You are community to me. I am especially grateful for you who have encouraged me or given me an idea I've used and used, or even stolen and adapted. These people include Steve Price, John Hodges, Carl Horton, Deb Guess, Beth Gunn, Cindy Edwards, and Mark Montgomery.

Again, I am grateful to the Hobsons—Flora, Rick, David, Patrick, and Cauley—for the use of their lake house for our writing. It was a pleasure to be in that space, and we are grateful for this generosity and support throughout the writing of this series.

Introduction

This book is designed for youth and their leaders and anyone else who knows or cares about youth and the communities they are building. It is for people who care about Christian community and all that might mean.

I know how I read recreation and community-building books. I read and use the games like a recipe book. I read, adapt, and use the recipes/games first, and then later I go back and read the pieces that might explain the background or other explanations. So this book is written for readers and leaders like me. Often the games are sprinkled in with the other text to hopefully push you and me to read the other "stuff" and think about the "whys" while we are doing the games and activities. Chapter 7 offers many games.

My "Top 10" games and activities are included in this book, as well as a few more. I've also included the "Mop 10," which are games that may sound fun, but they are not fun if you have to mop up after any participant or the entire youth group! I often call these activities "recreation from hell." That's how it feels for at least one person in these kinds of activities. I include them because some of what I have learned about community building I have learned because something did not work. These "not" games have been a teaching tool for me. But hear me say—PLEASE do NOT use these games. Take my word for it: They do NOT help build a group!

 The less than wonderful (mop) games or activities are distinguished by the "not" symbol.

 The positive games and other more useful activities are distinguished by a "star" symbol. These are also noted with a series of "gradings" for "debriefing."

D = You **may** debrief but don't need to
(game can be an end in itself).

DD = Probably the activity **needs** debriefing, but not a lot
(it can be an end in itself or a means to another end).

DDD = You **must** debrief, or many will miss the point
(a means to another end).

What I call "debriefing" is crucial to making the purpose of the game really happen. *Debriefing* means asking questions after something has happened in order to obtain useful information (see chapter 8 for more on debriefing). Without the use of debriefing, the game is just a game, and in many cases the game will be empty. It is in talking about the game that people realize that the community is being built and one can acknowledge the presence of the Holy Spirit in the game.

I pray that as you use this book, you and all who are with you will experience the presence of the Holy Spirit. God continues to teach me about the balances and power of individual relationships versus group relationships. The power of the presence of the Holy Spirit in recreation for me is awesome. God can work miracles for individuals and groups in and through recreation. We are truly re-created as God's children.

For you who have not ventured into working with groups and community building, you are in for a treat. For you veterans, may you continue to enjoy the adventure of self-discovery (and discovering others) and may you experience a new understanding and a richer relationship with our Lord and Savior, Jesus Christ. Acknowledging Jesus Christ in your recreation is an amazing and yet natural addition to any game or activity.

1
Group Building— Why Do It?

One of the most important ideas in group building is, if it's not recreation for everyone—it's not recreation.

Assumptions and Implications

☺ Games are something we play.

☺ Play is something we did or do as children.

☺ We are children of God.

☺ Jesus said "Truly I tell you, unless you change and become more like children, you will never enter the kingdom of heaven. Whoever becomes humble like this child is the greatest in the kingdom of heaven."(*Matt. 18:3, 4*)

Therefore: Games, recreation, and play can help us experience the love of God.

☺ Recreation is RE-CREATION.

☺ In recreation, we are being re-created to be who God calls us to be.

☺ Recreation helps us build common unities.

☺ Common unities build community.

Therefore: Recreation is community building.

☺ Youth need to find out and examine who they are.

☺ Youth need to experience acceptance and belonging.

Therefore: Youth need to participate in experiences that are positive, interactive, and safe, and they need to grow in and with a group of other youth and adults. Youth must have a safe place in which to explore faith issues and experience God and examine their relationships.

One way these experiences happen is through recreation. That is because recreation

☺ is interactive

☺ is re-creation

☺ is community building

- is a gift from God
- is a place to experience the community of faith
- is a chance to become a new person.

Therefore: Community building must be safe and inclusive; it must make good use of people and material resources, and it must be involving, purposeful, and Christ-centered.

Community building takes place when

- everyone is involved
- each person has a right to pass
- no one is ridiculed
- the presence of the Holy Spirit is acknowledged, honored, and welcomed
- there is a sense of accomplishment for everyone
- participants discover something about themselves and God.

Community-building activities are useful and appropriate if they meet the above criteria.

Now that we've put the tool of recreation in the proper perspective, we're ready to tackle the question, What is group building and why do it?

Assumptions and Implications

- People need and want to be accepted for who they are as children of God.
- People need to be encouraged to be more of whom God calls them to be.
- People need to be encouraged to give and receive and be involved in the life of a group or community.

Therefore: When these needs are met, *community* is formed.

Community building and *group building* are used synonymously here. We are about constructing, building, making, growing a group, and having community *happen*. We are helping a community form and a group become established. These are not utopian gatherings. Communities are people who come as individuals. A community is made up of individual people! People bring with them history, expectations, baggage, ideas, and hopefully a relationship with God. These are people who may or may not care about each other. They may not always like each other. They may struggle and face serious issues together. They love each other through growing edges and hard times, and yet they encourage each other.

Community is church. The story of the birth of the church in *Acts 2* is a story of people who are from different places and who speak different languages coming together. They received the gift of the Holy Spirit. The chapter ends with words of how they lived together and shared and grew together as church. In the best of all worlds, this connotes images of family and church as God meant them to be. *Acts 2:44* speaks of believers being together and having all things in common. One of the messages of this chapter in Acts is that the Holy Spirit came to the people when they were **T O G E T H E R !**

> ## Jesus said, "Where two or three are gathered in my name, I am there among them." *(Matt. 18:20)*

We need only to be aware of this. At the wedding in Cana, it wasn't just any party. The party happened because Jesus was there, and the people knew that. This is what we are about in group building: acknowledging the presence of God and the impact of Jesus in our midst. I often ask youth what difference it makes that we play games at church—how is it different from playing games at school or other places? *Acts 4:32–34a* says it simply:

Now the whole group of those who believed were of one heart and soul and no one claimed private ownership of any possessions but everything they owned was held in common. With great power the apostles gave their testimony to the resurrection of the Lord Jesus, and great grace was upon them all. There was not a needy person among them.

Community . . . Group . . .

In this book we are looking for ways

☺ to build *community* and *group*

☺ to help the community/group grow

☺ to realize that in growth there are times of slow growth, pruning, harvesting, reaping, death, going to seed, replanting, and new growth.

I will not spend a lot of time on these analogies, but I hope the reader will keep them in the back of the mind as this book is read. I hope these planting and growth images will help clarify the concepts of identity and belonging.

Two Basic Concepts

Young people bring with them a quest for *identity*. They long to find out "Who am I?" Along with this need, they are searching for a place to *belong*. They need a place to be accepted unconditionally. Youth long to find out "Where do I fit in?" Bill Myers, in his book *Theological Themes of Youth Ministry* (Pilgrim Press, 1987), says that as Christians we can push this one step further, and the question becomes "Whose am I?"

> **"Whose am I?" is a deeper, richer question. As Christians we live our lives seeking to learn what this means. What does it mean to be a child of God?**

We will explore these issues knowing that they are a lifelong quest. And we realize that developing skills in young people for finding the answers is important as we *all* continue to search, explore, and experience glimpses of what it means to live our lives as children of God. Who Are You? (see p. 8) enables participants to get to know not only themselves but others as well.

For community building or group building, the community must feel like a safe place. In a safe place, participants are able to share in at least two ways:

- ❂ to share something of the self—share strength or even a weakness (social, emotional, spiritual, or physical)

- ❂ to have a new experience that is shared with the group—that is, the game or activity is a place and time when a new story is built, and some new memory is made with others.

In other words, the youth give and get. Each person *gives* something to self and to the group, and reciprocally the self and the group *get* something. In the best of all cases, self-discovery and self-disclosure go hand in hand for each individual. When this happens in a community/group context, a bond is formed among people.

Gangs today are a clear example of young people who are on this search. The good news for Christians is that Jesus is about making us his gang. But the term *gang* often connotes something exclusive. This is where the "Jesus gang" image breaks down because God sent God's Son for all people, regardless of race, gender, socioeconomic status, and so on.

In the foreword of the book *Guerrillas of Grace*, Ted Lower speaks of Christians being guerrillas, people who are fighting for a cause they believe in.

There are two or three characteristics of guerrillas that give particular relevance to the use of that image to describe Christians. By any of our usual measures, guerrillas are a weaker force set against a superior and more organized power, a power which exerts both subtle and blatant pressures to conform. Such pressures are not commonly or quickly perceived or interpreted as oppressive, but frequently something in them is experienced as, at least, vaguely stifling to the spirit.

Guerrillas, then, are engaged in the battle to reclaim some territory, or some part of life, for a higher purpose, a truer cause. To wed guerrilla with grace suggests that the truer cause is God's kingdom. Since the "principalities and powers" are never completely "out there," but also stomp and rumble "within," a significant piece of the life to be reclaimed or liberated is the pray-er himself or herself. . . .

It is also important to note that guerrillas usually work in groups. In some fashion we never pray alone. We always pray toward someone and with someone—namely, whoever resides within us as teacher, friend, enemy, burden, brother, sister, spirit. However private our prayers may seem, we are still the cloud of witnesses when we pray (just as we are when we think or act). So, the prayers in this volume, though framed in personal terms, could easily be used as corporate prayers, and in many instances have been. The point is that both grace and guerilla are relational terms.

And finally, guerrillas are never quite so desperate as they are confident. They believe they are fighting on the winning side, in spite of any and all appearances to the contrary. We have to be exceedingly careful in even considering this characteristic, for abuses perpetrated by religious arrogance are all too evident and painful. Still, guerrillas are willing to give their lives, if necessary, because they believe in the cause for which they struggle, and which struggles in them, will finally prevail. Even so, the pray-er is always saying, one way or another, ". . . thy kingdom come."[1]

People join gangs because they are looking for a place to belong and want a purpose, a cause, a reason to be there. As a Christian community, we have that place to belong and our cause: We are a community of faith, wanting to live as children of God. We want to be that church described in Acts: sharing ourselves, growing together,

1. *Guerrillas of Grace*, by Ted Lower (San Diego, CA: Luramedia, 1984), pp. 7–8. Used by permission.

giving, experiencing, participating in the society—in the community.

This is the purpose of community building: to have a place of identity, a place to belong, a place to work for a cause, a touchstone for this whirlwind life we live, a place of growth in the Spirit of Jesus Christ.

A group-building activity or game has a product or result that is in addition to the value of the pleasure it gives to an individual who plays. That additional value is what the game or activity does for the individual within the group and for the group itself. For Christians, this value can be a microcosm of real-life Christian community. The community that is built is of value to the individuals within it and has value for what it is or can be as an active and interactive body.

Who Are You? (DDD)

Formation: pairs
Supplies: paper and pen for each person
Directions: Ask the person whose birthday is closest to today to be the first person to ask the questions. Tell this person she or he is to interview the partner by asking the same question ten times and getting ten answers. The interviewer should record the answers on the paper just as they are said. The partner should answer in short phrases, sentences, or single words. The answers can be serious or fun. After each person in the pair has interviewed and been interviewed, have the interviewers give their papers to the one interviewed. Debrief by having the partners discuss the roles listed on their sheets and which of these they like and dislike or why.
Value: Partners get to know what each partner thinks of her or his own self; participants recognize and share perceptions of self.

2

Theology, Competition, Language, and More

Assumptions and Implications

☺ Youth have loads of pressure to succeed.

☺ Church is a place to be what or who God calls us to be.

Therefore: Experiences at church need to be positive and wholesome, and we need to watch carefully the issues of winning and losing.

Obviously, theology undergirds this book. Any whys and purposes of what we do as Christians are theologically related. Think through all purposes of recreation and community building, especially of the deeper, even subconscious purposes of building a group. Why are you doing what you are doing? You may find this to be a highly theological question. Ask yourself and those with whom you work:

☺ What are you wanting to accomplish?

☺ What are the lessons—overt and covert—that are being learned, espoused, and practiced?

☺ What does doing any particular game with youth teach the youth?

☺ What is your style of leadership teaching the youth?

☺ What are these people taking home from these activities?

Everything you do, including the way that you do it, reflects some kind of theology.

Ask yourself:
Why am I doing this? Why are we doing this?

The answer needs to be something more than "Because it is fun!" Pure fun crosses the line of fun and becomes *joy* when we are doing community building. *Joy* is deeper and richer than fun. And a deep and meaningful and even difficult discussion may not be fun, but it can be joy-filled in its outcome.

Joy is also biblical:

"Rejoice in the Lord always; again I will say, Rejoice"
(Phil. 4:4, referring to a charge of how we are to live life together).

"... that my joy may be in you, and that your joy may be complete" *(John 15:11, referring to love and joy perfected in Christ Jesus).*

"... that they may have my joy made complete in themselves" *(John 17:13, referring to a portion of Jesus' prayer for his disciples).*

"My brothers and sisters, whenever you face trials of any kind, consider it nothing but joy"*(James 1:2, which tells us to face difficult times with joy).*

Even in the most difficult of youth-ministry or group-building situations, we are instructed to face these times with joy. Joy because that is where we are truly in touch with God, where it is deep and rich and meaningful.

Chuck Melchert, former professor at the Presbyterian School of Christian Education, did some research on Old Testament uses of the word *rejoice.* He found there are places in the Old Testament where *rejoice* could be translated as "to play with God."

The first question of the Shorter Catechism is "What is the chief end of humankind?" We find the impetus for all of our recreation in the answer:

To glorify God and enjoy God forever.

When we can look at recreation and community building through the eyes of this question and answer, perspectives are clear. The purpose of all of life, including any community building, is God-centered. All actions and interactions should be to the glory of God. The implications are limitless! So this Q & A becomes a guideline and a measuring stick for any community building we do. As we plan and lead recreation of any kind, we can ask ourselves:

> ### Does this help young people glorify God and enjoy God forever?

So what about recreation and competition? Today most young people must deal with competition and pressure from competition. They deal with pressures to be captain of the varsity team, achieve first chair in the orchestra, make the best grades, get in the best colleges, get the best job, make the most money, and live in the biggest house. The list is endless. The pressure to *succeed* is incredible. Pressure is *to do successfully*! The picture painted for youth is that they are striving to be at the pinnacle of some proverbial triangle. They must be *at the top* and be the *best* at anything they do!

The contrasting image we offer young people as Christians is a circle: Everyone is standing in a circle, connected equally. The image shows God calling us to be the best of who *God* calls us to be. This includes contributing to the whole of the community. We are called to be a part of community together, individuals contributing to the whole. The encouragement is that we be the best for God's sake. The encouragement is to be *faithful*.

Similarly, our culture gives youth enough to think about related to winning and losing and the pressures involved: making the best grades, getting in the best colleges, making the most money, buying the best car or house. The church should not be engaged in encouraging this same kind of performance behavior.

I believe the church needs to be a place where young people can be *re-created* to be who God calls them to be and be the best of who that is. The church needs to make clear that God does not compare the young person to anyone else. God is not keeping score. By just being their best, youth impact the community in wholesome ways. I don't think this is an extreme because it relates to the first question of the catechism: "What is the chief end of humankind?" Again, note that the answer is not focused on something we *do* but has to do with whom we *are*: "To glorify God and enjoy God forever." The focus is on God and on being who God calls us to be! The focus is not on doing and performing but on *being* and *enjoying*.

Sports and other games that require keeping score usually have winners and losers. Someone goes home with *more* points than someone else. One team *beats* another. One person *wins*, another *loses*. One team is *better* than another. Listen to this language! This is not God's language.

Footrace is a game that is an example of winner/loser theology (see p. 14). Elimination games such as Footrace have a similar exclusive theology. People who are *eliminated* are the losers. They are *out*. They do not get to participate. So we have to consider what the youth are learning when they are eliminated and are out of the game. Loser? Left out? Not as good as the others? Not as skilled? Can't score as many points? Won't get *chosen* next time? You know the list. Is this what they are learning at church?

Sports and many other games do the elimination thing. This may be their nature. The elimination thing happens and people WIN and LOSE! When we do sports with youth in church settings, we are obligated to talk about it. What did we learn? How does it feel to win and lose? How is this like life? How is this the same as or different from our faith work? Where is God in all this? What do we learn about life? We need to be conscious of all the facets of what we are teaching and what recreation is and what is being re-created.

There are some creative ways to reinvolve people who are eliminated and get them back into the game, such as in On Pon Clap (see p. 14). This is the *only* way in which elimination games and activities are acceptable! In addition, the only way sports, or any games that keep a score, are acceptable with youth in the church is if you help the group discuss the elements of working together and winning and losing! Debriefing is the key; it is discussed in this book in chapter 8.

> **It can be proven that a three-year-old understands the concepts of competition and a third-grader can explain it. Try it sometime: Ask a three-year-old to pick the best of something or tell you which one is better, smaller, taller, and so forth.**

For this reason and more, it is helpful to remove the word *team* from your vocabulary when talking to youth and youth groups. Team connotes competition. Even if no team competition is planned, use of the word *team* immediately makes young people think of competition. So any activity immediately takes on a competitive element when any group is referred to as a team. When you haven't planned for competition and the word *team* is used, you will have to deal with elements of competition somewhere in the activities just because of this language.

Watch it sometime. Play a game for fun. Don't say anything about winning and losing and watch what happens. The first group back or finished with the project will say "Yay!" and throw their hands in the air, or even say "We won!" This has happened time and time again with the game Lighthouse (see p. 15). This game has wonderful issues of trust to debrief. It is also fascinating to do this activity with a group and watch and debrief the *other* dynamics that arise from the group as they play—especially any issues of competition. (Most groups think this is a race or that getting back quickly is part of the activity.)

Sometimes competition can be healthy. It is healthy when the competition is to achieve a goal the whole group is working on.

Healthy competition is

○ when a group can work together toward a goal

○ when the object is to overcome some obstacle

○ when all are involved in coming to a positive solution.

The healthy question to ask is the following: What builds up individuals and enhances the community?

When Scripture uses words like *attain* and *the prize* and *the goal*, it is referring to the call of God in Jesus Christ. *Philippians 3:14* says, "I press on toward the goal . . ." but the verse and the paragraph do not stop there! The goal is not something we compete against each other for. The goal is life in Jesus. When we are doing group building with youth, we must have this same goal: life together in Christ Jesus and holding up and growing as the church. Some of this may seem like semantics. The point is, we must try to be consistent and uplifting with these activities with youth. So in this light, think about a couple of other concepts that promote competition and winning/losing:

○ prizes and awards

○ food games

Again, think about the purpose of games like Snoot Snoot (see p. 16). What is being taught? If you play with food, what are people learning about the value of food? It is irresponsible in our time to use food as a disposable toy. If the food cannot be used (as in *eaten*) at the end of the activity, do *not use it!* Sure, your parents' words echo: "Remember the starving children in China." With our world as small as it is, we *know* there are people in this world without food. We Christians should not play with our food. We don't have to go to China to find people who don't have food.

There are some activities (I wouldn't call them games) in which food is not wasted. It is eaten, and it is the object of the lesson. Some simulation games like Thirty-Hour Famine teach about hunger. These activities can be group building because different people have different experiences within the same group, and there is plenty to debrief, understand, and learn from each other and from the experience. One such activity is What's for Dessert? (see p. 16).

Concepts of waste and extras and expendable supplies like food can translate to almost anything that is wasted. This issue can be an ongoing discussion, an ongoing learning process, and a greater and greater challenge to be more aware of what we are teaching when we teach or lead or play games.

These concepts can be boiled down to two theological words:

○ stewardship

○ inclusivity

The verb *steward* means to take care of and manage. Being good stewards of what God has given us means that we need to work toward not wasting supplies and equipment. In addition, as leaders of youth, we need to model this.

For youth leaders, being inclusive means we are conscious of making sure everyone is included in games and activities.

Footrace

Formation: two or more lines of participants

Directions: On "Go," the first person in each line runs down to a specific marker, tags it, and runs back. That person tags the next person in line, who then does the same. The game continues until everyone in the line has run to the marker and back. The first line to get all their people to the marker and back wins.

⊘ = *Not recommended for group activity*

On Pon Clap (DD)

Formation: circle of players—at least four, as many as twenty

Directions: Teach the following moves and have everyone do them with you. Say the word and do the motion at the same time:

○ ON: Put one hand under your chin with fingers together but pointing in the natural direction to the right or left (right-hand fingers will point to the left, or left hand will point right).

○ PON: Similar to ON, but hand is on top of head; right-hand fingers pointing left, or left-hand fingers pointing right.

○ CLAP: Clap hands with fingers of both hands pointing in the same direction and toward someone else in the group.

Have the group practice these three moves together and note that the fingers are always pointing to someone. Right-hand fingers always point to the person on the left and left-hand fingers point to the person on the right.

Tell the group the game has three separate moves. The play

starts with one person who says the first word, "On!" and does the motion. The person she or he is pointing to says, "Pon!" and does that motion. The next person who is pointed to does the "clap" motion, but cannot say that word.

If someone messes up the motion in any way or says the word (*Remember:* the word "clap" is not to be said), or gets the sequence confused in any way, this person must become a "heckler."

A "heckler" comes out of the circle and stands, moves, or sits behind the circle and may "heckle" the group or individuals. The heckler may say anything to the people in the group—the only stipulations are that hecklers may not touch the others playing or obstruct their vision in any way.

The object of the game is to try to stay "in" as long as possible. Once someone becomes a heckler, the object is to try to get others to mess up and become hecklers too.

Value: Some concentration is required; all people are included in the game; it is a fast-moving game and a good icebreaker.

Lighthouse (DDD)

Formation: sets of partners standing against one wall
Supplies: blindfolds (can use lengths of material, bandannas, or hose or bright tights)
Object: for one partner to get the other blindfolded partner across the room and back safely
Directions: Explain the game before anyone puts on a blindfold. Tell them that the sighted partner must stand behind the blindfolded partner and hold the blindfolded person just above the elbows, firmly, with one hand on each elbow to guide them across the room, help them touch the wall, and guide them back to where they started. After they get back, have them switch roles so both partners experience being blindfolded and being the leader.
Variation: Tell youth that the sighted one may go over by holding on to the partner and may not talk on the way over. Then after they touch the opposite wall, they must come back by using only verbal instruction. So it's: Go over touch-no-talk and come back talk-no-touch.

Be sure to debrief this activity! (See chapter 8 for information on debriefing.)
Value: It requires trust; communication skills of different kinds are needed and can be developed; lots of transfer value in debriefing.

Snoot Snoot

Formation: relay lines

Supplies: small boxes of favorite cereals

Directions: Have the groups line up with their favorite cereals. On "Go," the first person in line sprinkles some cereal on the floor. This person bends down to blow air through her or his nose and blow the cereal across a line designated about three to five feet away. After the cereal gets across the designated line, the first person runs back to the group and tags the next person in the group to repeat the same task. The first group to finish getting their cereal across the line "wins."

Value: *None!* This is recreation from hell. Food is wasted, groups are competing to "win," and for what purpose? Germs are shared, and this game can be just plain gross!

⊘ *= Not recommended for group activity*

What's for Dessert? (DDD)

Formation: any formation where people are seated or standing around tables

Equipment: tables and chairs—enough for one table for every four to eight people; two old magazines for each person and masking tape, or some other kind of arm splint

Supplies: simple ice cream sundae fixings or any other dessert fixings that require personalizing the dessert before eating it

Directions: Set out the food on the tables so everyone can reach all the fixings. Tell the group to fix themselves a sundae—one each—but everyone must wait to eat until everyone has made a sundae.

After everyone has made a sundae, pull out the splints. Tell the group they need to help each other put the splints firmly on their arms. If you are using the old magazines, give each person two magazines. Tell the group to help each other tape one magazine snugly around each elbow so their elbows are splinted and don't bend. After everyone has a splint snug on each arm, give thanks for the food and tell everyone to enjoy their sundae.

The group will quickly find out without your telling them that it is impossible to feed themselves. They will have to feed each other.

You *must* debrief this activity (see chapter 8 for debriefing details).

Value: The need for others is clear; lots to debrief: the value of others and the symbolism of feeding each other is made clear.

3

Life of a Group

Assumptions and Implications

- ✹ We often don't have the privilege of seeing every day the youth with whom we work.
- ✹ The group of youth with whom we work can change from week to week.
- ✹ Community building takes *time*.
- ✹ A Christian community needs to be open.

Therefore: We need to plan carefully the hour or hours a group of young people have together.

If you ask a young person how long it takes to make a good friend at school, often the response is "about a month." Well, do the math. If it takes twenty days (four weeks of five school days) to make a good friend at school, youth programming has a lot of work to do. Using this formula, that comes out to *five months* of programming with a church youth group (one hour of programming each week, that means twenty weeks—five months). This lifts up the necessity of having some solid blocks of time in which community can be built. I believe we as church leaders of youth can do a lot more in our quality program of one hour than can be done in one day at school. But clearly we must spend major amounts of time early in the year with youth (early in the school year in most communities) to conscientiously work at making *community* happen.

It can take twelve to fourteen consistent hours just to form a group. That means twelve to fourteen constant *contact* hours. A retreat or conference is ideal for this. It can serve as a time to help your group build community in a concentrated block of time.

At the beginning of the year it is important to concentrate on doing some good solid community building. In fact, nearly *all* programming at the beginning of the year needs to be community-building oriented.

A good rule of thumb is to imagine yourself as the "new kid" who just moved to town. Everyone else knows each other, but you know no one. You want to fit in. You want to be accepted. You want to belong. How do you make an entry? As you imagine yourself as that new person, try to step in his or her shoes, and plan accordingly. With this in mind, remember that group building must be intentionally planned at the beginning of the school year *and* revisited every time someone new enters the group. The weight of group building is heavy at the beginning of the year. As programming moves to more content, group building is more and more woven into other activities until eventually everything you do is community building because the group gets used to and gets into operating and functioning as a group.

It is possible to have a different group of youth every week at a regularly scheduled event. That makes daily or weekly group building imperative. It becomes a ritual. A young person may spend one weekend with one parent in one town and the next with the other parent in another town. Continuity in group building is almost a thing of the past. But young people know that in youth programming there will be intentional times of group building and checking in with the community, they come to rely on this ritual and count on this constant experience of community.

As the year progresses, less direct community building is needed (unless a new member joins the group), because the group should know each other well enough that most anything they do together is and can be community building. In order for this to happen, the individual participants in the group have to know each other. Again, issues of *identity* and *belonging* come into play (see chapter 1).

Building a Community — One Year at a Time

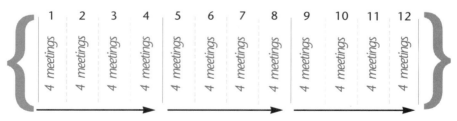

one-hour meetings / once a week / four times a month

For those group members who must come and go during the year, the consistency of some ritual of group building helps them check in and reconnect.

All this is really about timing. Timing is important in the life of a group. There is a "life" to the group in a single event of group building. It takes time to help the youth invest in each other and the group. Therefore *planning* any single event is important. Use the "Five Es," which I discuss in my book *Surveying the Land*:

- ✺ **E** ngage

- ✺ **E** ncounter

- ✺ **E** xplore

- ✺ **E** xpress

- ✺ **E** mpower

Plan sessions that involve the youth in using the Five Es, which can help develop the group's life.

These Five Es are themselves about timing: You can do with no less than five minutes for *engaging* and *encountering*, and you will need at least ten to fifteen minutes for each of the last three Es. I don't believe it is possible to do much group building in less than an hour. Two hours is really preferable if you want to help the group realize and absorb what they are doing as a community.

Cliques are groups of people who have formed a community, however healthy or unhealthy. They exclude other individuals or groups. They serve as a place of belonging for some and are in their own right a kind of gang. Cliques are not always bad. They may be a jumping-off place for other community building. A clique becomes destructive when it is disruptive in any way. Conversely, it may be necessary to work to creatively separate the members of a clique, to encourage the youth to make other friends, and in the most positive cases, to open the clique to incorporate everyone else.

In chapter 7, there are suggestions for moving people between and within activities so that these can be used to break up cliques.

4
Leadership

Assumptions and Implications

❂ For any activity, people need clear, concise instructions.

❂ Group building should include the leaders.

❂ Leaders set the tone for most activities.

❂ Selfless leaders have the interest of all people at heart.

❂ Youth learn theology from how we lead.

Therefore: As leaders, everything we do is an example and a model, and we must engage and involve *ourselves* in the group.

❂ Activities begin when the first person walks in the room.

❂ Do it! Then talk about it!

❂ Think about what you want the individuals and the group to leave with.

❂ Youth learn from how leaders lead.

Therefore: Group building cannot happen unless leaders prepare and look ahead, juggling these implications and more!

Leading for the Glory of God

Leaders can look to the first question of the Shorter Catechism:

What is the chief end of humankind?

In the answer we find the impetus for all who lead groups in recreation:

To glorify God and enjoy God forever.

This becomes our guideline for styles and methodologies of leading young people in any kind of recreation. Our goal is that all actions and interactions will be God-centered and done to and for the glory of God. The implications are limitless!

When we think about leadership of recreation in general and community building, specifically, we become the hosts of the youth and the group. We are the enablers of the community building. Self must be put aside, and we must function as vessels and instruments for God, which God uses to make God's community. We do this for God, for God's glory, not our own.

When these concepts slip or get out of kilter, the *glory*, the purpose and center of our leading, becomes selfish and is for ourselves, our own growth and advancement. Not only does God know this, but the youth we lead know it. Leading recreation is other-centered. The *other* includes youth, the group, and God. It is God-centered recreation.

Again, we come back to earlier discussions of the place and nature of competition. I'm talking about the kind of competition that pits individuals and groups against each other and where someone or some group is made to lose, where one person or group is glorified, and where one person or group wins or beats another person or group.

You as a leader are an instrument of God! You are an enabler in the most positive sense of the word. You are the vessel through which the group is built and the community is opened to each other and to the movement of the Holy Spirit. Remove any ego needs related to being in front of a group! You cannot be an instrument of God if you are the one seeking recognition and glory. In group building, we are about glorifying God first and the group next.

Leading through Participating and Preparing

A good leader finds ways to *participate*. You engage the youth by engaging yourself as the leader in the activities. This is not "Pied Piper" leadership. This is *engaging* and *interactive*.

Part of being prepared as a leader is being ready for the youth as they walk in the door. These are *hospitality* issues. A good host or hostess is ready and has prepared ahead of time for what the youth need as they walk in, is prepared to make them feel at home, and is working to make them feel like they are a part of a group. The host or hostess has already thought through the following:

- ❂ What do they need?
- ❂ What do they expect?
- ❂ What do they feel or need to leave feeling?
- ❂ What do they think or need to leave thinking?

Leading through Believing in What You Do

Remember, *your* energy is contagious! As you are leading a game, the group can tell if you are invested in it or care about them. By the same token, they can often tell if you are *putting on* an attitude and are not really interested in them or the activity. In other words: *Be genuine! Be involved!* And *believe* in what you are leading and what you are doing with the group!

Leading Briefly but Clearly

As a leader, try to use as few words as possible. Don't make a group stand and listen to long explanations before getting into a game or activity. Have them do the activity as you explain it, so they see how the game works. My friend and mentor Glenn Bannerman would say: "Do it and then talk about it." Get the group into a formation and explain what needs explaining and let them have the game. Give them the game as quickly and as simply as possible.

Sometimes it is helpful to say something like "let's do a pretend round" or "let's practice this once." Before you and the group know it, they are in the game. It doesn't matter if it is a pretend round—keep going with the game.

By the same token, if you need to start over, you can. Give more explanation if needed. Make sure everyone is clearly understanding you. It's okay to say, "Let's try it again." Remember, performance is not the issue. You are playing a game or an activity. This is not a performance or a test. Play the game!

The adage **K.I.S.S. (Keep It Simple, Silly!)** certainly applies when you are giving instructions for any game or activity, as does the ever-popular **"Just do it!"**

Leading Is Not Entertaining

Real recreation and community building is *not* entertainment. Entertainment implies something to watch. It is passive. Entertainment is watching TV or some kind of performance. Community is not built there. We must engage the young people to get them *involved* in the group building.

Shared leadership is wonderful and a great model for young people to experience. Having youth and adults share in the "up front" leadership of any activity is something from which everyone can benefit. Balance is the key to shared leadership. A youth and an adult sharing leadership is wonderful, but a host of youth and adults leading something is borderline entertainment. When the group has many leaders to watch or follow, it often becomes easier for the participants to sit and watch than to get involved in the activity.

Leaders should be leading; they should not be showing off or doing some kind of show and tell. The focus must be on being instruments to *engage* the participants in the activities for *their* benefit. Showing off or having friends lead to make a leader feel or look popular does not help build a group or encourage community. When a leader chooses to have a host of help, those who are not getting to be the so-called leaders may be thinking, "How can I be on stage?" What kind of community building is this? In addition, the group you are trying to involve in the activities, the group you are trying to build, will often opt out of the activities. It becomes more fun to watch what is going on than to participate. It is no longer clear who the leader is or what the leader is leading. The only thing that is clear is that a bunch of people are on stage and there is a lot to watch.

In other words, a good leader does not need a platform, figuratively speaking, every time he or she is in front of group. A good leader has the group's interest at heart and is functioning out of a need and mission to glorify God and encouraging others to do the same.

Here are some additional tips for leaders:

- ☻ Make eye contact—look at everyone.
- ☻ If speaking to more than forty people, consider using a microphone.
- ☻ Greet the group—if necessary, wait until all are quiet.
- ☻ Give concise and clear directions.
- ☻ Do it, then talk about it.
- ☻ Be aware of specific cultural issues.
- ☻ Be sensitive to special needs or disabilities.

Remember that you can take the competition out of relay games by doing any one or all of the following:

- ☻ Keep score by giving four- or five-digit numbers to those who "win" their relay round.
- ☻ Have the groups trade some members after each relay. Trade the third and fifth persons in each line, or have the back half of each group move to be in front of the line next to it.
- ☻ Say "Go when you are ready" instead of "On your mark, get set, go."

Making these changes puts the emphasis on fun and takes the pressure off by reducing the perceived need to win.

Dealing with Cheating

In school and in most of life, people who cheat are regarded as having done something wrong. They have broken a trust. They have violated rules or a covenant. They have broken an honor code. In games and activities, cheaters can be disruptive and frustrating to the leader and others involved in the game. Cheaters are people who look for a way to get ahead or win a game by playing outside the rules.

Sometimes cheating can be addressed by reviewing the group's covenant for being together. You may need to establish consequences for this kind of bad behavior or other disciplinary contracts or actions. The youth involved may need to be debriefed after such instances.

I'd like to propose another view. You as a leader must *also* have almost a "third eye" as you observe instances of "cheating." It may be that a cheater is really someone who is fun-loving and is just bored with the game as it is. This "cheater" may simply be getting creative with the play of the game. Only if you are using this "third eye" can you see beyond the activities and to the real *issues* the youth are dealing with and what the cheaters are saying to you and the group.

In these instances, cheaters *can* be creative game players who aren't "cheating" to get attention or to disrupt the activity. These young people are bored and are looking for ways to spice up the game. Look at what they are doing—they may be suggesting ways to enhance the game, to make it more exciting. Consider whether you can adapt the game and incorporate their ideas so that the game has an added dimension of fun, and maybe joy, for everyone.

It is your responsibility as leader to keep control of the game and not give control to these kinds of game players. These people are not difficult to deal with if their energy can be channeled creatively back into the game before the behavior gets disruptive.

Remember, the opposite of a cheater may be a quitter. Quitters have gotten *out* of the game. They have quit. It is easier to keep a "creative" person *in* a game than to get a quitter back into a game.

Having a Plan B

As a leader, you must have a "Plan B," a list of alternatives for a particular time or sequence of activities if your original plan is not working. Some leaders make Plan B by overplanning, having too many games to do. This will work only if the leader is able to sense where the group is and how all the interpersonal and interactive dynamics are working. The leader must also have a sense of the work of the Holy Spirit in their midst. When it is time to move to another activity, *move*. Don't feel like you have to play or continue a game just because it is on your list.

My friend and mentor Glenn Bannerman says, "Cut the game off at its peak." Leave them wanting more, more of that game and more recreation in general. This alone can help the developing community. There is a chemistry that the Holy Spirit is developing in this flow of activity.

The leader must be cognizant of this movement, of what is happening within the community. A sharp leader is ready to capitalize on this. A sharp leader is ready to capture the energy and feelings and move the group into the next activities that will prepare youth for a deeper commitment to each other. This environment affords an awareness of the movement of the Holy Spirit among them. These flow issues are discussed in chapter 7.

You as leader must intuit the needs of the group—before you plan, as you plan, and as you are leading each game or activity. Planning ahead will help you see and hear the group's needs and be able to adapt. Use Plan B if needed, and pull all the pieces of what is happening together. Plan B must be a healthy plan, not an activity that exploits or leads to uncomfortable feelings. On the Spot is an example of a "not to do" activity (see p. 26).

The leader must also know when another game is needed to drive a point home. When needed, do it. The leader must be aware of what needs to be debriefed. Debriefing is discussed in chapter 8, but suffice it to say for now that many points of community building will go unnoticed by the group as they enjoy a game. The leader must be aware of these points and help the group revisit them.

Characteristics of a Positive Leader

- ☺ anticipation—anticipates needs and where the group is going
- ☺ friendliness and hospitality—is the consummate host/hostess
- ☺ intentionality—knows what is happening and when it is happening
- ☺ gives energy
- ☺ participates with the group
- ☺ leads, does not entertain
- ☺ makes eye contact—looks at the group so they know the leader knows
- ☺ gives of self—showing and sharing energy
- ☺ leaves a feeling of wanting more
- ☺ never belittles, embarrasses, excludes, pokes fun at anyone,

especially anyone who is different from him or her (e.g., belongs to another racial-ethnic group, economic background, or has a disability)

✪ engages the participants, moving them beyond passive entertainment to involved group building

On the Spot . . .

Formation: none

Directions: In a group, ask anyone having a birthday in December to come forward in front of the group. Have the birthday people sing "The Twelve Days of Christmas" as a small group.

Value: *None.* I call this recreation from hell. Those having a birthday are put on the spot and might be laughed at.

⊘ = *Not recommended for group activity*

5

Needs of Young People in Group Building

As with any youth activity, the first question to ask about group building with young people is

✪ What do the youth need?

The second question is

✪ What is needed for these individual young people to make a group or community?

Finally, ask

✪ What are youth taking home (figuratively speaking)?

Youth need a place to at least get a glimpse of God's realm, a glimpse of an experience of being whole. In a society that is fragmented and not centered, young people need to experience this wholeness that has to do with being Christ-centered and a part of a Christian community. Being part of a Christian faith community will, we hope, mean the youth will be able to move outside into the larger community knowing they have this Christ-centered foundation.

The book *The Roots of Who We Are,* by Rodger Nishioka, outlines "Characteristics of Young People." Youth leaders might benefit from using this or any similar list of developmental characteristics of youth, and asking themselves,

If this is true for youth, what do they need to have happen in order to experience community?

Ask yourself this question any time you hear a true statement about youth or youth culture.

There is a whole set of questions to be answered when one asks, "What do youth need?" (Much of this is dealt with in my book *Surveying the Land,* which is part of this series.) So tweak this question of what youth need and ask, "What do youth need in order to help them build or be a part of a faith community?"

Assumptions and Implications

✪ Early adolescents need activity.

✪ People learn best by doing.

- Early adolescents work best in groups of fewer than five.

Therefore: We need to offer chances for experiential learning in small groups.

- Most adolescents, and especially early adolescents, float back and forth between being able to think concretely and being able to think abstractly.

- Our faith is full of symbols and the abstract.

Therefore: We need to encourage young people to stretch and to think abstractly.

- Hearing stories, we can visualize the people and the events.
- Telling stories about ourselves, we are sharing something of ourselves.
- We get to know people by hearing something of what they have done.

Therefore: Story sharing—youth to youth, adult to youth, and youth to adult—is an important part of self-disclosure.

- When we experience a game with someone else, we develop some memories in common with them.
- Common memories are a bond.
- Memories are shared by sharing stories.

Therefore: Creating memories helps with community building.

- Churched young people are sometimes an intellectual bunch.
- Churched young people often can give the right or correct answer.
- Many young people are not asked or encouraged to internalize or personalize faith issues and responses.

Therefore: We need to ask young people, "What do you think or feel about . . . ?" and "How does _____ affect you?"

Conversely:

- Many youth today did not grow up in the church.
- We in church work and youth ministry can no longer assume that young people know the stories of the Bible.

Therefore: We must share the faith stories and help young people apply them to their lives today.

☺ We do a lot of "stuff" with youth.

☺ We often talk "about" our faith.

☺ We ask youth to think theologically or look at biblical issues and concepts.

☺ We also often omit the most important question, "So what?"

Therefore: We need to ask, "So what?" to get youth to reflect on what they've participated in and make the transfer to their lives tomorrow, their interactions with others, and their growing relationship with Jesus Christ.

Youth need

☺ to talk about their faith

☺ to be pushed to think abstractly

☺ to be asked questions

☺ to have fun

☺ to get to know others, themselves, and God

☺ to share their own story

☺ to have a safe place

☺ to be accepted

☺ to belong.

6

Timing, Safety, and Logistics

Assumptions and Implications

- Young people grow physically at different rates and speeds.

- Physical abilities of any group of young people vary as much as the young people themselves.

- Many youth are not aware of their physical abilities, their strengths, or their weaknesses.

Therefore: We must plan to meet different needs and yet plan for youth to be physically safe.

- Self-esteem is developing in young people.

- Many youth are self-conscious.

- Many youth care a lot about what others think of them.

Therefore: We need to make all our activities emotionally safe for young people.

- Location, setting, and facility are important aspects of planning.

- Physical obstacles can be hard to plan around and can be dangerous.

- Youth function best in a place where they are comfortable and safe.

Therefore: Space, location, and other physical facilities are important considerations in planning.

Ask yourself a series of questions as you look at and plan for the time with the youth for developing community:

- What is the time frame? Are you planning for an intense forty-five minutes? Are you planning for ninety minutes or more?

- Where are you in the life of the group, and what are the needs?

- How well do the youth know each other? The answer to this question impacts how much time is needed for each activity.

Leaders must always have an eye for safety. It is important to watch for sharp objects and corners, slick surfaces, obstacles, and anything else that might cause injury. Special precautions are necessary with adolescents for several reasons:

- ✪ They are growing fast. This offers flexibility and yet can also mean they are awkward and not completely aware of their abilities and disabilities.

- ✪ There will be an enormous range of strengths and abilities within one group of young people. Extremely coordinated and strong young women will be in the same group with young men who have not yet hit any kind of growing spurt. The reverse is also true. The same is true for height, agility, and other physical characteristics.

- ✪ Young people are often self-conscious about their bodies, their abilities, and how they "measure up." It is important that we not put them on the spot in terms of physical ability.

Safety must also include emotional safety. People must know they are not going to be made fun of, put on the spot emotionally, or left out in any way. Emotional safety issues overlap some of the theological and competition issues discussed in chapter 2. We must always be conscious of who is being glorified and, conversely, who is being left out or put down. Lick and Stick is an example of a game that is undesirable because it infringes on the emotional safety of young people (see p. 32).

The parallels of glorification are helpful in realizing the impact of safety issues related to sexuality and sexual misconduct. When any question arises that concerns sexuality, ask yourself, For whose glory are we, or am I, doing this? These highly important issues *of risk management* are discussed at length in the book *Growing Leaders*, by Bob Tuttle.

When a new challenge is put to a group, it is important to encourage the young people to participate in the challenge, but it is also important to give them the option to pass or suggest another way of participating. Do not push anyone into activities he or she is not comfortable with. Encourage participation. If you have the flow planned well, most everyone will naturally be encouraged to participate.

Physical logistics are a part of the issues of safety. Think through the possibilities that a room or a play space offers you and the group. It is difficult to plan for recreation of any kind in a facility you have not seen, so check out new facilities such as retreat sites ahead of time, if possible.

As you are planning, consider

⚙ time of day

⚙ time allotted for activity

⚙ size of room or space

⚙ size of group

⚙ obstacles in room

⚙ supplies needed

⚙ equipment needed.

Ask yourself "set-up" questions:

⚙ Where is the front of the room?

⚙ What objects in the room can and can't be moved?

⚙ Where are the places that people can get hurt?

⚙ Where is the space people can move around in?

⚙ What set-up changes with chairs and tables and so on need to happen?

⚙ How can I make these changes happen easily?

Lick and Stick

Formation: pairs of boys and girls
Supplies: pack of lifesavers for each pair
Directions: On "go" the girls rip open their pack of lifesavers, lick each one, and stick it on their partners' faces. If any fall off, the girls lick and stick again. The first pair with all the candies on the boy's face wins.
Value: *None!* To touch someone's face is deeply intimate. Adolescents can be self-conscious with concerns about acne and this kind of intimacy. Food is wasted. Boys and girls don't need to be paired in this inappropriate kind of touch. Germs are shared. It's a sticky mess. The so-called winner gets nothing of value.

⊘ = *Not recommended for group activity*

7

Flow—
Games We Play

Assumptions and Implications

☺ Community building involves sharing oneself.

☺ Community building requires risking oneself.

☺ People need to feel safe in order to risk.

Therefore: Build one activity on another and develop a system of moving smoothly into sharing (specifically) and group building (in general).

☺ Adding an individual to a group can be intimidating.

☺ Consolidating groups changes the original group's dynamics.

Therefore: each time a group has people added to it or taken from it, do an activity that will encourage individual sharing.

The word *flow* has already been used in this book, but let's look more closely now at what it means in youth ministry.

☺ Flow is being concerned with numbers of people and how they are grouped from activity to activity.

☺ Flow is arranging people and formations of a group—in lines, circles, and so on.

☺ Flow is the result of your decisions about all of the above.

One important key to having a good flow of activities is to have something planned for everyone to do from the minute he or she walks in the door. This way you will have the group hooked into an activity by the time you need to speak to them. Make sure there are clear directions for what they are to do so they can move into the activity easily. The message you are giving them is that you have planned for them. There is no question about your preparation. They know they will be engaged.

In my first book, *Surveying the Land,* which is about planning and youth ministry, there is a lot of discussion about "form follows function." This is an important concept in considering flow. If the leader has not thought about and planned for the functions of the group and their purposes in being together, there can be no form. That is why the subject of "flow" comes up at this point in this book: We have already worked through issues of theology and other elements of building a group. These issues are the *functions* of group building. We can work on flow and form now that we know the functions of the time together and the group.

Another factor in planning flow is helping the youth with self-esteem questions. Obviously youth don't come in the door literally asking self-esteem questions, but if youth are concerned about belonging and identity, having a prepared place for them to interact when they walk in the door says to them, "You have a place here."

There is flow in

- formations of groups of people — lines, circles, and so on

- numbers of people in groups— twos, threes, eights, twelves, and so on

- kinds of activities

- energy levels

- theme progressions.

Ask yourself, as you plan flow

What is the next activity, and how does it relate to the last and the next in terms of

- physical energy

- mental energy

- self-awareness

- other-awareness

- awareness of God

- interactions with self, others, God

- the interweavings of these interactions?

Let's assume that the leader knows the purpose of the group's time together. But in planning each meeting, leaders should remind themselves of it by asking: What is the *purpose* of our time together? What *activities* will make that purpose happen? What is the logical and helpful *flow* of those activities? What additional activities may need to be added to ensure that the purpose of our time together really does happen? The first and most integral part of figuring out this flow of the activities has to do with the group's formations. What are the formations the individuals need to be in to interact with others? How do you move from one formation to another?

> If a leader considers these issues of purpose and flow for a planned activity, there will be community building.

Think about it. If you have an activity with the youth in groups of three and then move to an activity that requires groups of eight and then back to an activity with the whole group and then to one with groups of four, the participants may begin to fear what is coming next. There is no rhythm to what is happening. The activities, instead of the purpose, are driving the agenda. If you move participants more logically from activities that require groups of two and then four and then eight, everyone will feel more comfortable.

For moving individuals into groups, here are some general rules:

☸ Never have participants count off. Some youth will scramble to get in their friends' groups.

☸ Never pick teams or groups. This is an antiquated grade-school method that singles out the best and the worst, and one or two people will spend the rest of time together thinking, I was chosen last.

Working with older adolescents, groups of six to eight are good for discussions, and a ratio of six to eight youth to one adult is ideal.

Working with early adolescents, groups of three to four are best for discussions, and a ratio of three to four youth to one adult is ideal.

Think about your old multiplication tables: two to four to eight to sixteen—these transitions are smooth and easy. The reverse works well too. Odd numbers are sometimes more difficult. Eight is often an ideal number in working with groups. Eight in a group is great for games and interactions in activities, and many games can be played in groups of eight. Three or four in groups helps relay activities move fast, and people don't have to wait.

It also to helps to think geometrically:

- ❂ Lines move easily to circles.

- ❂ Lines or circles split in half easily.

- ❂ Lines or circles can be made
  into a square or a triangle.

- ❂ A circle can be divided into two lines.

- ❂ Lines facing each other can move into partners
  (each person in one line is paired with the person
  directly across in the other line).

Look for appropriate times to move everyone into one large group.
Try to plan at least two activities within the same formation. For
group building to take place, some self-disclosure needs to happen in
each formation. Participants need to see, feel, or think about how they
connect to others by sharing something of themselves and some kind
of activity with those people. The community needs to be a place that
is safe to discover something about the self. Perhaps the sharing is
about a strength or even a weakness (social, emotional, spiritual, or
physical). The community needs to be a place that is safe to share
something about the self with the group. Individuals share
experiences through the game or activity.

Both self-discovery and self-disclosure happen here. Stories are
shared, and new stories are made and experienced. History is shared
and history is made. This happens with individuals and with the group.
In the Christian community the touchstone is Jesus Christ.

Awareness of this happens because people have been brought
through the flow of activities. They have been brought into a safe
place to share, and they have been opened to the spirit of sharing and
also to the Holy Spirit.

Groups

- twos ➡ fours ➡ eights ➡ the whole group
- random whole group ➡ twos
- random whole group ➡ circle ➡ lines ➡ small groups
- lines ➡ groups ➡ whole
- lines ➡ circle ➡ groups ➡ whole
- low energy ➡ high energy
- high energy ➡ low energy

Ideas

Ideas for random mixer questions:

Ideas for random groupings:

Ideas for getting people into lines:

Ideas for getting a group into pairs:

Ideas for getting a group to mingle:

Ideas for getting a group into a line or a circle:

Ideas for pairs to do together:

Ideas for fours to do together:

Ideas for eights to do together:

Ideas for a group in a circle:

Ideas for groups in a line:

So what are some of these activities that provide a healthy flow? What are the activities that a leader can use to build one activity on another that will provide an opportunity to develop a system of sharing and group building? The answer to these questions is right here. The remainder of this chapter offers just such activities. But before you browse through these activities, let's review once again my debriefing grades.

Debriefing Grades

D = You **may** debrief but don't need to
(the game can be an end in itself).

DD = Probably the activity **needs** debriefing, but not a lot
(it can be an end in itself or a means to another end).

DDD = You **must** debrief or many will miss the point
(a means to another end).

Who Goes First?

Sometimes someone is needed to go first. To relieve the pressure of figuring out who goes first in an activity or game, here are two rules of thumb:

1. Take a volunteer—whoever wants to go first in a group can go first.
2. Give a guideline that will help the group figure out who should go first, such as moving the
   - person whose birthday is closest to today
   - person wearing the most blue
   - person with the longest hair
   - person to the right of the person with the darkest eyes

Risk and Energy Levels

As you are thinking about flow of the formations, it is important to think about the flow of the risk levels, both physical and emotional risks. Asking youth as soon as they come in the door to line up does not instill trust in each other, the leader, or the activity! Most everyone needs to warm up to these kinds of interactions. Unless everyone in your group knows everyone else, before starting any new game or rearranging people during the activity, make sure the group is encouraged to share at least their first names. Even for the one new person in the group, each time you change the formations of the games, ask the group to share their first names and one other tidbit of information about themselves. This self-disclosure is sharing oneself, learning about oneself, and learning about others. When we share our stories and hear others' stories we are developing history with each other. This history building helps develop community. Activities such as What Is Your Favorite? are good for trust building and self-disclosure.

Some Additional Tips for Leaders

Do not put anyone on the spot. Do not put any pressure on new people in the group. Ask everyone to share names if you are having one person share his or her name. Ask everyone to share anytime you are doing any kind of sharing.

Anytime you need to show by example, it is important to have a volunteer. Again, don't put anyone on the spot because that does *not* help to build community. If you have warmed up the group with the appropriate flow activity, there will be plenty of volunteers. Then those wishing to opt out can do so.

Leaders need to give some thought to the flow of energy levels, as well as risk levels and types of formation. We need to consider the energy levels the individuals bring in and the energy levels we want to generate with the group as a whole. Middle-schoolers will need to burn up more physical energy than senior-highs.

Think about what is going on with your young people and plan accordingly. If you know your young people have had a hard week or time period in school, you will want to start the programming slowly and probably gently, but move to something high energy where they can blow off some steam and use more physical energy. In this scenario, they probably will need to burn up physical energy, but they may not be willing to spend much time or energy with a lot of "heady" programming since they have been studying hard.

Similarly, there are appropriate levels of risk you should ask the individuals and the groups to take. You cannot ask any individual or the group to risk anything physical or emotional without making it safe to risk. As each step of the group's movement (two to four to eight) happens within the flow, the group will be more and more willing to share themselves, to risk.

It is critical that the leader be an astute observer of all movement in both the small groups and the whole group, for more is moving in the groups than the physical movement of the people. These sharings that people do—sharings of self, perspective, or ideas—are also windows of opportunity for the movement of the Holy Spirit. It is one thing to plan for all the physical movements; it is quite another to be aware of the Holy Spirit's movement from person to person, person to group, and group to group. If the planning has been thorough, allowing for emotional, physical, and spiritual movements, the leader will be cognizant of the faith and theological issues that are arising and which ones need to be highlighted, brought out, discussed, and debriefed.

Again, think through the purpose of the outcome you're striving for. Why are you doing all this? The flow of the formations and flow of the energy of the Holy Spirit within the group will help you get there. Leaders must always be aware—must watch, listen, and sense—that they are working for and with the Holy Spirit.

The question to ask yourself as a leader, and maybe to ask the group, too, in a debriefing setting, is this:

✪ What difference does it make that we do these activities at church and that Jesus Christ is in these activities?

OR

If Jesus were physically here,

🌼 what would he contribute?

🌼 observe?

🌼 think about our activities?

What would you want to . . .

🌼 say to him?

🌼 ask him?

What do you think he would . . .

🌼 contribute to the group?

🌼 want to say to us?

🌼 want us to do?

Ask yourself as leader the following questions:

Have the individual youth and the group been moved well into group building?

Has this been done logically and to the benefit of the individuals and the group?

Activity 1
Ideas for Random Mixer Questions (D)

1. What is the best vacation you ever had?

2. Where would you go if you could go anywhere for a two-week vacation, and money and time were not issues?

3. What is your all-time favorite movie?

4. What's the best movie you've seen in the past six months?

5. If you had $100,000 you could not spend on yourself, what would you do with it?

6. What is the most valuable thing you are wearing, and why?

7. What's your favorite subject in school?

8. What's your most difficult subject in school?

9. Where is your favorite place to be in your house?

When appropriate, tailor questions to particular situations with your group, such as the following:

1. What is the best activity we have done with our youth group in the past year?

2. What is one hope you have for our youth program?

3. What is something our youth group could do for someone else?

4 What do you really like about our church?

5. What is one thing you would like to change about our church, and why?

Value: Sharing pieces of themselves and their own histories and hearing about other people helps youth understand other people.

Activity 2
Ideas for Random Groupings
Forced Choices (DD)

Think of four categories of ideas or information, such as those listed below. Read them off to the group, and have them stand in one of the four corners or four areas of the room according to the one they choose.

1. What kind of music do you like best?

   Country

   Rock

   Alternative

   Classical

2. What is your favorite kind of ice cream?

   Chocolate

   Vanilla

   Strawberry

   Chocolate chip

3. What is your favorite children's movie?

   Jungle Book

   Robin Hood

   Aladdin

   Beauty and the Beast

4. Identify with one of these cartoon characters (have participants chose one from each set of cartoon characters):

   Pooh

   Tigger

   Owl

   Rabbit

   OR

   Mickey

   Minnie

   Donald

   Daisy

OR

Cat in the Hat

Green Eggs and Ham

Sneetches

The Grinch Who Stole Christmas

Each time the youth switch to another group, ask them to find share their name with one or two others in the group and explain why they chose that group or made that decision

Note: Do not use examples of identification such as sports teams, political issues, or anything that would divide the group emotionally or cause them to take sides on hot issues unless you want to debrief this activity. That would make this activity a **DDD**.

Value: It forces choices, mixes people up, gets people into listening and moving, and allows some self-disclosure.

Variation: Have newsprint on the walls displaying various questions for which people may write answers as they come into the room:

☺ What was the best part of your week?

☺ What was your favorite game as a child?

☺ What do you admire in others?

☺ What makes for a good friend?

☺ When you have free time, what do you like to do?

☺ What does community mean?

☺ What is recreation?

☺ Why do recreation?

Questions can be tailored to the topics of the planned group-building events, such as community issues and sharing gifts. Identify minor or sub-issues you want your group to deal with. Tailor the questions to what the group needs to deal with.

Value: It provides a place to interact from the moment a youth walks in the door; it provides a place to express an opinion and for simple self-expression; there are no wrong answers; it is a discussion starter.

Activity 3
Ideas for Getting into Lines
Lineups (DD)

Have the youth stand in a line by certain topics by asking them to line up by one of these factors:

- ⚙ last two digits of their phone number, from 01 to 99

- ⚙ eye color, lightest to darkest

- ⚙ birth dates, month and day (not year) in chronological order

- ⚙ color of clothing, in rainbow order: red, orange, yellow, green, blue, indigo, violet, black, white (you will probably need to post this list of colors so the group can see the order)

Or make up your own topics.

Variation: Ask youth to get in a circle instead of a line. This will help the lineups seem a little less graduated in value (as in biggest to littlest). The whole group will be able to see each other. It can also help facilitate the games/activities that follow.

Caution: The younger the youth, the less you should use physical characteristics. Many young people, especially early adolescents and young women, are self-conscious about their shoe size or height or other physical attributes, especially when they think they might have to measure up to others.

Value: It gets people mixed up, regardless of clique attachment; the group has to work together in a nonthreatening way; everyone has to interact with at least someone.

Activity 4
Ideas to Get a Group into Pairs
Back to Back (DD)

Tell the group: Stand back to back with someone. Using your back, express

- How do you do?
- I'm glad to see you
- What's your name?
- sadness
- happiness
- anger
- fear

. . . and then some kinds of food:

- hot fudge sundae
- popcorn
- bacon frying

Ask the youth to switch partners from time to time.

Value: It can help mix up cliques or pairings that always seem to happen; everyone interacts; allows safe, simple touch; can be as active as the leader wants; is a good icebreaker.

Puzzle Pieces (DD)

Make puzzle pieces by cutting cards (from a deck of cards or the like) in half. Use half as many cards as there are people (for instance, ten cards cut in half for a group of twenty). Give each person half a card. Have the youth walk around and exchange cards. At a predetermined signal (ring a bell, cling a glass, turn off music that is playing), tell the youth they must find the person with the other half of the puzzle they are holding. After they find their other half, give the group a question such as one of the "random mixer questions" in Activity 1 to answer with the partner.

Variations:

1. Print a question from Activity 1 on the cut cards, so that when the pieces get together, the question can read and be answered.

2. Use one side of old cereal boxes as the puzzle. Put a question on the back of each cereal box side; then cut it in half or even fourths.

Value: It makes individuals in the group interact; forces simple exchanges between two people; permits nonthreatening self-disclosure; mixes people, is an icebreaker.

Activity 5
Ideas to Get a Group Mingling
Traffic Jam (DD)

With the youth standing in any random order or configuration, tell them you are going to call out a series of directions and they need to follow them. Give the following directions in pairs or trios; that is, give two or three commands in a row.

- ❂ Take two steps forward.

- ❂ Turn a quarter turn either right or left.

- ❂ Take three steps sideways.

- ❂ Take one step backward.

- ❂ Take three steps sideways.

- ❂ Turn a quarter turn right or left.

- ❂ Take two giant steps forward.

After every second or third move, have the youth face someone and shake hands or answer one of the random mixer questions (see Activity 1). If participants do not know each other, have the pairs share names and another random mixer question.

Value: This is a simple, nonthreatening way to get people moving with some simple interactions; okay for introverts; quick.

Touch Blue (DD)

This activity is a variation on the game Twister. With youth in any configuration (sitting in chairs, random, standing), have them reach out and touch someone according to the instructions listed below. Make it clear that everyone must touch something that is on someone else. Tell them to touch someone who

- ✪ is wearing blue

- ✪ is wearing white socks

- ✪ is wearing glasses

- ✪ is wearing white tennis shoes

- ✪ has a color of eyes that is different from yours

- ✪ has hair longer than yours

Variation: Tell everyone to put his or her

- ✪ right hand on something blue

- ✪ right elbow on something that's not yours

- ✪ left knee on something little

- ✪ left big toe on something rubber

This variation makes the activity a little more like the game Twister. Now and then have them introduce themselves to the person they are connected to at that moment.

Value: It provides simple, nonthreatening touch and simple interactions; and stretches people beyond self.

The ideas listed in Activity 2 for random groupings and Activity 4 for getting a group into pairs can also work to get a group mingling.

Activity 6
Ideas to Get People into a Line or a Circle

If your space is large enough, set up chairs ahead of time in the particular configurations you need: groups of three to four, lines of six, a big circle. Do a few activities as the group comes in and then invite them to sit in the chairs that are already set up.

Chairs in a Large Circle (D)

Prearrange the room with chairs in a circle, leaving a wide space in the middle. Have the first several activities in the middle of the room. When you are ready for the group to be in a circle and be seated, tell them to remember who they are next to as the previous activity ends. Then tell them to sit in a chair next to one of these people.

Chairs in Lines, Small Circles (D)

Before the group comes in, clear the room and put stacks of perhaps eight chairs against the walls. Work the larger group into groups of four to eight. Using Activity 8, have the group pick one person from their group to go and get a stack of chairs and bring it back to the group. Have everyone then sit in a chair with their group. Then think geometrically as you move them into the next formation needed, such as by

✪ having two groups face each other in two lines

✪ bringing three pairs together to make a circle

✪ having a group of eight open out into a line paralleling a particular wall

✪ splitting a group of eight in half and having the two groups face each other in two lines

✪ splitting a circle in half and having the two lines face each other

Value: It provides easy ways to move a group into another formation; it's more comfortable for participants to be instructed to move to a chair already set up than to have to make a decision about where and when they move, "cold" and uncertain.

Activity 7
Ideas for Pairs to Do Together
Partner Tag (D)

Tell the pairs this game involves only the two of them. Tell them the person in each pair wearing the most blue will be "it." "It" is to count to ten while the other person walks away from "it." When "it" gets to ten, "it" walks to tag the partner. When "it" tags his or her partner, that person is the new "it," and the game starts again with "it" counting to ten. Emphasize that everyone must walk! Tell the pairs to go when they are ready. The game goes until the leader says stop. **Value:** Promotes high energy; gets people moving; allows simple interaction with one other person and safe physical touch.

See also **Lighthouse (DDD)**, described on p. 15, and **Who Are You? (DDD)**, described on p. 8.

Activity 8
Ideas for Fours to Do Together
Partner Tag Squared (DD)

This activity is the same as Partner Tag (see Activity 7) except that it's done in fours. After playing Partner Tag, have the pairs find each other and tell the partners to hook elbows. Ask them to face another set of partners, but hold on only to their own partner. Tell them the pair that is wearing more green is the "it" pair for the first round. Tell them the game is the same, only no one can let go of the partner. When you see that they understand, tell them to go when they are ready.

Value: It promotes high energy; gets people moving; requires work with a partner; allows simple interaction with three other people; makes good transition for groupings moving from twos to fours.

Pleasant Playful Childhood Memories (DD)

In groups of three to four (up to, but no more than, six), ask everyone to think back to when they were children. Ask them to pick an age between five and nine when something good was happening. Ask them to recall one specific story from that time. It can be something that happened just once or something that occurred regularly, such as every year or every week. Tell them they will have two minutes (or up to five minutes) each to share their pleasant childhood memory with their group. The amount of time has to do with how much depth you want the groups to go into and how much time you want to take. Tell them you are going to give them a minute to think about the story they want to tell. Then they can listen to the other youths' stories while they wait to tell their own story. Designate which person in each group should go first, and then, going around the circle to the right, have each person tell their story.

Value: It is fun to recall happy childhood times; self-disclosure can be simple or complex; can lead to deeper sharing of self and history; builds community to share and hear other youths' stories; can relate to stories for children in Scripture.

Activity 9
Ideas for Eights to Do Together
Machine Charades (DD)

Ask the groups (groups no smaller than three or no bigger than sixteen can work for this activity) to think of a machine they can portray in a charade. Tell them that everyone in the group must have a moving part in the machine, and anything that moves is considered a machine. Give the group a couple of examples. Use easy examples, such as a car, which could have four people doing somersaults as wheels, several people jumping up and down as pistons between the front two wheels, someone crawling along as the driver's seat, and a driver sitting on the seat shifting gears.

Value: It gets creativity going and is interactive; individuals have to work together to decide what to do and how to do it; it's fun to watch other groups; has low physical risk; helps physical expression.

Architecture Charades (DD)

The groups are to portray different kinds of buildings or structures and what happens in them. Make sure youth understand they are not to act as the people in the buildings, but only the building itself.

Building ideas:

- Ice cream parlor
- Bank
- Fast-food restaurant
- Football stadium
- Playground
- Roller coaster
- Church

Value: Presents creativity challenge and is interactive; youth have to work together to decide what to do and how to do it; helps physical expression.

Commons (D)

Formation: two or more groups of people

Directions: Tell each group they need to come up with a movement and a sound that can be done by everyone in the entire group. They are to make up a sound and a movement that can be done at the same time. Then each group will teach the other groups their sound/motion. After each group has made up their own sound/motion, have them share theirs with the other groups, one group at a time. Make sure each group knows all the other groups' sounds/motions by reviewing all the sounds/motions.

Tell everyone they are to huddle with their own group and decide on one of the sounds/motions they have learned that all the groups will do together. The object of the game is to try to figure out which sound/motion the other groups will do, so that all groups will do the same one.

After the groups have had a moment to decide, have the groups come back together with everyone facing the center. On the count of three, have all the groups do their sound/motion at the same time. The groups that are doing the same sound/motion join each other. Go again and again until all the groups are one big group.

This game is the opposite of the old Rock, Paper, Scissors game. Instead of working to beat the opponent, the groups work to try to do the same thing.

Value: It gets creativity moving and is interactive; participants must work together to decide what to do and how to do the activity; gets the entire group to interact; moves separate groups into one large group; provides silly/fun element.

Activity 10
Ideas for a Group in a Circle
Group Juggle (DD)

Formation: standing or sitting in a circle

Supplies: several sockballs. A *sockball* is three to four socks balled into another sock and tied off. You can also roll a couple of stockings into another stocking and tie it off. The advantage of using a sockball over another ball is that there is little or no pressure to catch the ball. It is soft, doesn't roll away if it's not caught, and it won't hurt anyone.

Directions: The object of this activity is to establish a pattern by tossing a sockball around the circle. Ask youth to sit with their hands in their lap. Give the sockball to one person and tell that person to toss the sockball to someone across the circle. Tell the tosser to remember who they tossed it to. The person who receives the sockball then tosses the ball to someone else. After people have tossed the ball, they put their hands behind their back to show that they have had the ball. Everyone receives the ball only once. The last person to receive the ball should be the first person who tossed it. You may need to tell the group that it doesn't matter if they don't catch the ball. It's okay to pick up any dropped balls and put them back into play.

Have the group toss the ball around the circle again twice, using the same pattern. Then add a few balls to see how many they can keep in the air.

Value: group has to work together; can be a name game; nonthreatening ball toss; lots of variations

Variation: *Call Ball*—For the first times around the group, have the person who receives the ball say his or her first name out loud and have the circle repeat the name all together.

I Sit (DD)

Formation: circle of chairs with one more chair than the number of people

Directions: The game starts on either side of the empty chair. Tell the group there are three moves in this game. The first starts with someone on either side of the empty chair moving to that empty chair. That person says, "I sit!" The person who was sitting beside that person follows him or her into the new empty chair and says, "I sit in the grass!" The third move is the next person who was sitting beside them who follows into the newly emptied chair and says, "I sit in the grass with my friend" and says the name of someone else in the circle. That person named comes over and sits in the empty chair. The chair that person left is the new beginning chair: "I sit . . ."; ". . . in the grass"; ". . . with my friend _____!"

Variation: Instead of having the group sit in chairs, mark the floor with masking tape or some other marker to designate their spots.

Value: It ensures that everyone moves; can be a name game; doesn't matter how many people anyone knows; can be good way for one or two new people to get to know other names; can have strategies to figure out; can move people to next game while sitting next to people they didn't start with.

Shuffle Shuffle (DD)

Formation: circle of chairs

Supplies: a chair for each person plus one extra chair

Directions: Everyone sits in a chair. Ask for a volunteer to stand in the middle of the group, leaving one more chair empty. The object of the game is for the person in the middle to try sit in one of the empty chairs while the others shuffle into the empty seats to try and keep that person out of the empty seat. The people on either side of the empty chairs shuffle right or left into the empty chairs. If the person in the middle does manage to sit in an extra chair, the person to his or her *right* must stand up and try to get into another seat.

But explain the safety value: If the person who gets into the middle doesn't want to be there or if that person gets frustrated with being in the middle, she or he can say "Shuffle! Shuffle!" and everyone must move across the circle to another seat.

Value: It ensures that everyone moves; can be a name game; doesn't matter how many people anyone knows; can be good way for one or two new people to get to know other names; can have strategies to figure out; mixes people.

Shuffle Toss Shuffle (DD)

This activity is Shuffle Shuffle (see above) with an added dimension.

Formation: circle of chairs

Supplies: chairs (one for each person and one or two extra chairs), a sockball

Directions: Play Shuffle Shuffle first, and then give a sockball to someone seated in the circle. That person tosses the sockball to anyone else seated in the circle, and that person catches it. The person in the middle can now try to catch the sockball too. If the middle person catches it, the person who threw it goes into the middle. This game moves very fast. In addition, if the person in the middle can tag the person with the sockball before it is thrown, the person tagged becomes the person in the middle.

So in this game there are three ways to become "it," the person in the middle. As in Shuffle Shuffle, there is a new "it" if the person in the middle manages to sit down. Then the person to his or her right goes in the middle. If the person with the sockball is tagged, that person becomes "it." If "it" catches the sockball as it is tossed, then the person who tossed it becomes "it."

Value: It ensures that everyone moves; can be a name game; doesn't matter how many people anyone knows; can be good way for one or two new people to get to know other names; can have strategies to figure out; some simple and yet funny coordinations required, but no particular skills; fun way to mix people.

All the games listed in Activity 10 are important because they get people interacting and mix up seating arrangements (that is, people end up not sitting next to the people they came with or are familiar with). They also offer simple communication and help the walls come down.

See also **On Pon Clap (DDD)**, described on p. 14, and **What's for Dessert? (DDD)**, described on p. 16.

Rolling Along (DD)

This game is for groups of six or less. Hand out dice, one for each group, and a list of questions. See the examples below for questions that incorporate the numbers **1** through **6**. The list should contain one of these sets of six questions, or six similar questions. A volunteer goes first, roles one of the dice, reads the question with the corresponding number, and answers the question.

Examples:

✪ What is the **1** best gift you have ever given?

✪ What are **2** things that make for a really good friend?

✪ What are **3** places you like to go?

✪ What is one thing you do "b4" you leave the house each morning?

✪ What are **5** characteristics of God or Jesus that you like or admire or appreciate?

✪ What's the best movie you've seen in the past **6** months?

OR

- ⚙ What does *1 Corinthians 12* have to do with group building?

- ⚙ What does *Acts 2:1–4, 40*, say about how we should live?

- ⚙ What do you think about *John 3:16*?

- ⚙ What are some joy issues in *John 4*?

- ⚙ In *Philippians 2:4–5*, what does "rejoice" mean?

- ⚙ How was Jesus treated in his hometown as described in *Mark 6*?

Note: Very little equipment is needed for these games and activities. To add to discussion, point out how little these activities cost for your group to do.

Value: Promotes self-disclosure and simple sharing; can be a short or longer activity; can be an opening activity for deeper sharing; there are no wrong answers.

Activity 11
Ideas for Groups in a Line
Lions, Tigers, and Bears (DD)

This activity is a variation on Rock, Paper, Scissors.

Formation: two lines of people facing each other, with a line marked off fifteen to twenty feet behind each group

Motions:

❂ Lions: Put hands on either side of your face with palms open forward like the mane on a lion.

❂ Tigers: Curl fingers slightly in front of you with arms bent, crouch a little.

❂ Bears: Standing on tiptoe, stretch arms above the head and curl fingers slightly.

Directions: As two groups stand in two lines facing each other, designate a line between them that makes the center of activity, and explain the game, teaching the motions first. Have the groups repeat in loud voices: "Lions and tigers and bears!" Teach the motions for each animal and have them say the phrase again and do the motions at the same time.

The Rock, Paper, Scissors parallel is this: The lions overpower the tigers, the tigers overpower the bears, and the bears overpower the lions. Have the group practice the motions and think about the order a few times. Give groups a couple of minutes to huddle with their group and decide which animal they are going to be as a group. Have the two groups line up in the middle of the room facing each other. On "Go," the groups all say and do together the words and motions: "Lions and tigers and bears!" and then their own chosen animal group (lion, tiger, or bear) on the fourth count. The group that overpowers the other group tries to tag members of the other group before the second group can get back behind their line. Anyone who is tagged becomes a part of the other group.

Value: It makes youth interact, listen to each other, and work as a group; can be high energy; requires mental and physical energy and expression.

Telephone Pole Shuffle (DD)

Formation: two groups facing each other in one line, or standing on one pole

Supplies: Using masking tape, mark off a line long enough for the whole group to line up on it. Mark a second, parallel line four to six inches away from the first. Or, if you know of a telephone pole lying on the ground or a length of sidewalk curb nearby, this will work too.

Directions: The object of the game is to move both groups from where they are on the "pole" to the same place on the other end of the pole without anyone on the pole falling off. Players must work together to help their group and the other group move on the pole.

Variation: Make the formation an "L" with each leg of the "L" an equal length. Have one group stand on one leg of the "L" and the other group on the other leg of the "L".

Value: People work together; has slight physical challenge; everybody wins.

Blind Run (DDD)

Formation: two lines of people distant from each other across a clear space (room or field) with no holes or obstacles

Directions: Explain the game first. People in one line will hold their hands up, shoulder height, palms facing out. Tell these people they are the bumpers. Ask them what the purpose of a bumper is, and have them articulate the positive role of a bumper. Tell them two to five people at a time will close their eyes (it may help to use blindfolds) and run across the clear space into the bumper arms at the other side of the room. Have two to five volunteers from the nonbumper side of the room take one step forward. Say, "Put your blindfolds on and go when you are ready." The bumpers will catch them. The bumpers may talk if it helps the runners. When a runner gets to the bumpers, the runner becomes a bumper too. After everyone who wants to has run from one side of the room into the bumpers (remember, all don't have to run), have the runners go back to their side of the room. The runners become bumpers and the bumpers become runners.

Variations: Tell the bumpers they can't talk or make any noise in the first round, or tell the runners they are to do a slow jog. After each side has jogged, go another round and do a run. Then if the group can handle it and the trust is high enough, have the runners run fast. (You may need to remind the runners they are trying to run to the bumpers, not through or over them.)

Value: It is safe, with low physical risk; allows self-chosen amount of risk; addresses trust issues.

Balloon Trolley (DD)

Formation: lines of people—at least three per line, but no more than twelve (sixteen is possible, but very difficult)

Supplies: nine-inch balloons or larger (balls will work, but are more difficult)

Directions: Establish a walking course around the church or playing area. It needs to be a course that can be walked without having to crouch or squat. You can mark the course on a makeshift map or tag the course with self-adhesive notes or other markings. Stairs and playgrounds are acceptable within the course. Ask the group to blow up enough balloons so there is one between each of the players standing in a line. Have the group stand one behind the other, facing forward. Ask them to put a balloon between each player. Describe the course, and tell them they are to walk the course and come back, without touching the balloon with their hands or arms.

Variations: If you have more than one line, send them on different courses. Or have them do the same course from opposite directions: Mark the course's halfway point and have the line reverse at that point so the caboose is the head and the head is the caboose.

Value: People work together; it is safe, with low physical risk; addresses trust issues.

What Is Your Favorite? (DD)

This activity involves asking an open-ended question such as those listed below. Each participant must answer the question and share why it is important.

What is your favorite

- dessert
- place in your house
- hiding place when you were a kid
- movie in the last year
- possession
- pastime

OR

My favorite (sport, movie ever, vacation ever, subject in school, place to be, TV show) is _____.

Value: There are no wrong answers; sharing the answer is safely sharing a part of the self; they get to know others by hearing their answers.

8

Debriefing

Assumptions and Implications

- ✪ Recreation can be an end in itself or a means to another end.

- ✪ Interaction in games or other recreation can be a microcosm of life.

- ✪ Young people often participate to participate and may not see these nuances.

Therefore: Debriefing—asking questions—after a recreational activity can help young people see the multilevel values of recreation.

Debriefing is important if you want to turn any recreation event or activity into a Bible study or to ensure that the participants know that there is theology in what you have been doing. You cannot assume that people today see or understand the connection between games or recreation and faith or God or the community being re-created!

Debriefing helps the participants be aware of and own the activity and their interactions (or lack of interactions) during the activity. It helps the youth begin to move their learnings from the recreation event itself to life—to see how they are re-created!

After several interactive games, it is important to use a debriefing process such as the one described below to help define, enhance, and hold up the learnings of the individuals and the group. It is important to stop and examine what was done, and how and why.

Debriefing Process

The first step in debriefing is to remember, as individuals and as a group.

Recall—State the facts about what happened, what you did or saw. Recount what happened—"The facts, ma'am, just the facts."

- ✪ What happened? When? How?

- ✪ What were your frustrations? likes and dislikes? joys?

Identify—Where do you fit in? Name the roles you played.

- ✪ Who played what roles, as individuals and in the group?

- ✪ Who did you identify with?

Claim—Share your thoughts and feelings about what you saw and experienced.

- What did you think about the game (or activity or movie or whatever)?

- How did you *feel* about interactions? about others? about yourself?

- What did you think or feel about what you did or what happened to you?

Restate—What are you learning from these activities?

- What did you learn from this game?

- What did you learn about . . . yourself? others? interactions?

- Why did things happen as they did?

Relate—How does this relate to Scripture or theology?

- How is this game (or activity or movie) like your relationship with God and the church?

- How does the Scripture passage relate to the game?

- How does this impact or influence your relationship with God?

- How does this impact or influence your faith?

Connect—How do these learnings connect to today, right now?

- What did you learn about yourself? about others? about God? about how we need to interact or live our lives?

- Why did we play these games (or do these activities)?

- Now what? In light of all this, what are we to do? How are we to act? to respond? to be?

- What does this passage and activity say about tomorrow? or about everyday life?

This debriefing is best done with groups of fewer than eight, although it can be done in larger groups. People will have more chances to share and articulate their individual learnings in groups of three to five people than in larger groups.

Caution

- Anytime you ask early adolescents to talk about their faith in these ways, you are asking them to think abstractly! Early adolescents are predominantly concrete thinkers. They need to be stretched in this way, but it is not easy. Be patient and ask questions.

- Do not ask yes/no questions. Ask, What happened? How? Why? Ask, "How is talking about your faith like . . . ?" Ask, "Why do parents want you to go to church?" Do *not* ask, "Do you talk about your faith?" or "Do your parents make you go to church?" Yes/No questions get yes/no answers.

A young man once told me, "You can't ask people 'why?' questions. They don't know why they do things!" I strongly disagree. We do need to ask people "why" questions! "Why" questions are theological. "Why" questions are deep questions. So it is important to first ask *what* happened and *how* it happened. Then move to *why*. People may be able to see the why after they have discussed or seen the what and how.

Don't get bogged down in this process. Listen! Pose a recalling question to begin with and you may hear them identify and claim other pieces. Make sure they have touched on the first three debriefing steps (recall, identify, claim) before moving to the last three (restate, relate, connect). If they have not done the first three steps—both as individuals and group—they will not be able to fully reflect on the meanings of the activities that will move them and their learnings beyond the time frame of the activities.

A simple way to debrief a group quickly is to ask four questions:

1. What happened?
2. How did it happen?
3. Why did it happen?
4. So what?

"So what?" is not a rhetorical or cynical question. It is important in making the transfer to life beyond the game or activity and especially life beyond the individual and the community at the moment. We often do young people a disservice by playing games and activities without helping them make transfers to life today. Another way to state the fourth question is, "What difference does it make?" What difference does it make tomorrow that we played this game today? It may be a variation on "Why did we play this game?"

Still another version of debriefing is to ask the group to finish these sentences:

❂ I think . . .

❂ I feel . . .

❂ I plan to . . .

This encourages youth to reflect on thoughts and feelings about the event, and asks them to look or think ahead to what it is they are taking from the event.

Debriefing is important if you want to turn any recreation event or activity into a Bible study or to ensure that the participants know that there is theology or purpose in what you have been doing. I repeat: You cannot assume that people today see or understand the connection between games or recreation and faith or God or being re-created. It doesn't hurt to ask these questions:

1. What did we do?
2. Why did we do it?
3. What did you learn?
4. So what?

It is especially important to debrief any activity that does not go well. Karl Rohnke, of Project Adventure, in a 1995 workshop, proposed a principle he called "FUNN": Functional Understanding is Not Necessary. He explained that you can even program failure because it allows you to try! It helps with "I can't" and the need to do okay. "Success is made up of failures," he said, and this is called "failing forward."[1]

But you cannot "fail forward" if you do not have some means of getting some learning from an activity that failed. Even the best of activities have pieces that could have been done differently or better. We learn from those pieces. In these situations and in using recreation as a group-building tool, recreation is a means to another end. The "other end" is the building up of the body of Christ.

What Is Recreation?

Recreation can be—an end in itself! A means to another end!

As you plan, keep in mind that recreation can be both an end in itself and a means to another end. To get to this "other end," first think of exactly what that end is. Then think: What are the dominoes that have to fall to get to that place? Think creatively. What games can be combined or adapted or reimagined to make a new game that leads to that end? What biblical insights and theological reflection can come from this game or activity? If the answer is *none*, then check out *why* you are doing the activity!

Young people today might say about community building:

☺ Talk to us, and we can overlook.
☺ Show us, and we can recall.
☺ Include us, and we really get it!

1. Karl Rohnke, 1995 Project Adventure workshop in Montreat, North Carolina.

TELL ME—
. . . I FORGET
SHOW ME—
. . . I REMEMBER
INVOLVE ME—
. . . I UNDERSTAND!

Consider the statistics given below about retention of information. I believe that these statistics from the early 1980s are now rather conservative. When we think about how many stimuli young people are exposed to today and how difficult it is to assimilate so very much information, these statistics are conservative.

People retain . . .

10 percent of what they *read*

20 percent of what they *hear*

30 percent of what they *see*

50 percent of what they *hear* and *see*

70 percent of what they *say* and *write*

90 percent of what they *say* as they *do*![2]

We need to work on the 50 percent, 70 percent, and 90 percent segments! We need to help young people experience the love of God with others. We cannot expect them to read about it, hear about it, and even see it. To really understand what the church is about, they need to experience Christian community.

---

2. *Teacher Training Manual,* edited by Frances Blankenbaker (Ventura, CA: International Center for Learning, 1982), p. 64.

Closings

Assumptions and Implications

✪ Youth need Christian ritual as a part of group building.

✪ There is security in ritual.

✪ Prayer is one way of communicating with God.

✪ We leave something out for youth when we don't pray with them.

✪ Closure to any activity is important because it seals the experience.

Therefore: Having a prayer or other similar ritual as closure for the group's time together is critical.

Simple closures can help pull together the experience of group building. If the debriefing or any other aspect of the group building has been difficult in any way, it is important to bring all the issues to God in prayer. In doing this, we not only ask for God's help, but we model for young people what is important in relating to God.

Closing is

✪ simple touch

✪ healthy ritual

✪ intentional connecting with each other

✪ intentional connecting with God

✪ prayer

Basket Weave

Formation: circle with everyone standing side by side
Directions: Tell the members of the group to put their right hand in front of the person to the right. Ask them to put their left hand in front of the person to the left. Cross "leftovers": That means your left arm goes over the hand in front of you.

There should be a hand by each person's hand for each person to hold. Tell the group members to hold that hand loosely. Point out to the group that everyone is standing in a circle, but everyone is *outside* the circle.

Tell them to lift up the hand they are holding, take a small step forward, duck under the hands that are held in front of them, and pull their hands down behind the people on either side of them. You may want to explain that the key to this is holding hands loosely and rotating the shoulder so the clasped hands can come down behind the backs of the people.

Ask the group to observe that everyone is now standing *inside* the circle. Close with prayer.

Value: Everyone is connected; provides an excellent visual symbol of being woven together and standing inside a circle.

Thumbs Right

Formation: circle with everyone standing side by side
Directions: Tell the members of the group to hold their arms out and turn their thumbs to the right. If everyone turns their thumbs to the right they can slide their hands into the hands of the people beside them. Point out that everyone is holding someone's hand and is being held by someone. Close with prayer.

Value: Permits visual learning; is a simple circle activity.

Open Circle

Formation: circle with participants standing side by side
Directions: Have the group hold hands in a circle. Have two people let go of their hands as if there is a space for one other person.

Chose one of the following and tell the group this space is

☺ for those who could not come

☺ for the new people who might come into this group next time

☺ a symbol of the space that Jesus Christ occupies in our midst

Value: Provides a meaningful visual learning and symbol.

A p p e n d i x
Programs for All Age Groups

Name of Activity _____

Purpose _____

Theology _____

Kind of Activity_____

Flow—Place in Flow _____

Directions _____

Age Group_____

Abilities _____

Energy Level _____

Logistics _____

   Setting _____

   Materials _____

   Supplies _____

   Equipment _____

   Facility/Location _____

Safety _____

Debriefing _____

_____

Supplies for this activity are kept _____

_____

Five Es of Planning an Event[1]
Engage

Encounter

Explore

Express

Empower

---

1. *Surveying the Land*, by Lynn Turnage (Louisville: Bridge Resources, 1997), p. 43. Used by permission.

Resources

Bannerman, Glenn Q., and Robert E. Fakkema. *Guide for Recreation Leaders,* Revised and Expanded. Louisville: Bridge Resources, 1998.

Bannerman, Glenn, LeeAnn Konopka, and Beth Gunn. *Brite Tites.* Loveland, CO: Group Publishing, 1997. ISBN 1-55945-497-0.

(Games and activities with hose/stockings, for all ages. Very helpful, low-cost, functional, multipurpose uses for hose/stockings/tights for most any recreation setting or need).

Maguire, Jack. *Hopscotch, Hangman, Hot Potato, and Ha, Ha, Ha.* St. Louis, MO: Fireside Books, 1990. ISBN 0-671-76332-6.

(Old and new games for all ages and groups—good introduction to kinds of games and leadership.)

Maness, Roger, Kenny Shackelford, and Don Washburn. *The Playbook,* 1995. Available at Cumberland Presbyterian Resource Center, 1978 Union Avenue, Memphis, TN 38104; 1-800-333-2772.

(Resource games and other group-related activities. Good for *all* ages!)

McGill, Dan. *No Supplies Required: Crowdbreakers and Games.* Loveland, CO: Group Publishing, 1995. ISBN 1-55945-700-7.

(Good group-building and miscellaneous games; some Scripture references.)

Nishioka, Rodger. *Rooted in Love: 52 Meditations and Stories for Youth Ministry Leaders.* Louisville: Bridge Resources, 1997. Item #095535.

(Devotionals for leaders in youth ministry.)

Nishioka, Rodger. The Roots of Who We Are. Louisville: Bridge Resources, 1997. Item # 095530.

(Basic how-to's of the theology, of youth ministry.)

Presbyterian Youth Connection. *Getting Connected—Presbyterian Youth Connection Congregational Guide.* Louisvillie: PC(USA), 1996. PDS 70-250-96-206.

(Planning helps, theological basis for youth ministry, ways of organizing, using the five intentions.)

Presbyterian Youth Connection. *Twenty Program Designs for 6th–8th Grade Youth Groups.* Louisville: PC(USA), 1996. PDS 70-250-96-207.

(Includes tips/articles for leaders and twenty program designs for youth. Relevant and fun!)

Presbyterian Youth Connection. *Twenty Program Designs for 9th–12th Grade Youth Groups.* Louisville: PC(USA), 1997. PDS 70-250-97-014.

(Includes tips/articles for leaders and twenty programs for senior highs. Great hot topics!)

Rice, Wayne. *Up Close and Personal.* El Cajon, CA: Youth Specialties, 1989. ISBN 0-310-52491-1.

(Group-building ideas and activities).

Rohnke, Karl. *Bottomless Bag, Again!?!* Dubuque, IA: Kendall-Hunt, 1991. ISBN 0-8403-8757-1.

(Games and activities; faith issues and debriefing not included).

Rohnke, Karl. *Bottomless Baggie.* Dubuque, IA: Kendall-Hunt, 1991. ISBN 0-8403-6813-5.

(Games and activities; faith issues and debriefing not included.)

Rohnkee, Karl, and Steve Butler. *Quicksilver.* Dubuque, IA: Kendall-Hunt, 1995.

(Games and activities; no faith issues or debriefing included.)

Rydberg, Denny. *Youth Group Trust Builders.* Edited by Stephen Parolini. Loveland, CO: Group Publishing, 1993. ISBN 1-55945-172-6.

(Activities for community building; some require equipment.)

Schultz, Thom, and Joani Schultz. *Kids Taking Charge: Youth-Led Youth Ministry.* Loveland, CO: Group Publishing, 1991. ISBN 1-55945-078-9.

(Good how-to book for basics and start-up issues; not much long-range information.)

Talbot, Mary Lee, editor. *Guidebook for Youth Ministry in Presybterian and Reformed Churches.* Louisville: Geneva Press, 1988. ISBN 0-664-25026-2.

(Overall guide; includes how-to's, PC(USA) information, five intentions, resources.)

Turnage, Lynn. *Surveying the Land.* Louisville: Bridge Resources, 1997. Item #095531.

(Basic how-to's of organization for youth ministry.)

Tuttle, Bob. *Dealing with Crisis.* Louisville: Bridge Resources, 1997. Item #095536.

(Helps for leaders in youth ministry.)

Miscellaneous— Other Great Resources

The Kids Multicultural Art Book. Charlotte, VT: Williamson Publishing, 1993.

Hands Around the World. Presbyterian Youth Connection Leader. Free quarterly publication.

(Annual Recreation Workshop. Montreat, North Carolina. First full week in May. Information available from 1-800-572-2257.)

About the Writer

Lynn Turnage is an Associate Director of Programming at the Montreat Conference Center in Montreat, North Carolina. An elder at Black Mountain Presbyterian Church in Black Mountain, North Carolina, Lynn has also served as Director of Youth Ministries at Preston Hollow Presbyterian Church in Dallas, on the faculty of the Presbyterian School of Christian Education in Richmond, Virginia, and on the staff of General Assembly in the Youth Ministry office in Louisville, Kentucky. She holds a master's degree in Christian education from the Presbyterian School of Christian Education. Lynn lives in a little yellow house with a big black dog and enjoys time with friends and dancing, and has an addiction to chocolate.